Essential COOKING SERIES

COMPREHENSIVE, STEP-BY-STEP COOKING

Rice & Risotto

HINKLER
BOOKS

HINKLER BOOKS

Essential Cooking Series: Rice & Risotto
First published in 2009 by Hinkler Books Pty Ltd
45–55 Fairchild Street
Heatherton Victoria 3202 Australia
www.hinklerbooks.com

Disclaimer: The nutritional information listed under each recipe does not
include the nutrient content of garnishes or any accompaniments not listed
in specific quantitites in the ingredient list. The nutritional information for
each recipe is an estimate only, and may vary depending on the brand of
ingredients used, and due to natural biological variations in the composition
of natural foods such as meat, fish, fruit and vegetables. The nutritional
information was calculated by using Foodworks dietary analysis software
(Version 3, Xyris Software Pty Ltd, Highgate Hill, Queensland, Australia) based
on the Australian food composition tables and food manufacturers' data.
Where not specified, ingredients are always analysed as average or medium,
not small or large.

ISBN: 978 1 7418 5708 5

10 9 8 7 6 5 4 3
14 13 12 11 10

Printed and bound in China

Contents

An introduction to rice and risotto

Labelled as 'one of the world's two most important food crops', rice is the staple food for a greater number of people than any other known plant. From its place of origin, it travelled to many lands and became embedded in the cuisines of many nations, creating the national dishes identified with them: the risottos of Italy, the paellas of Spain, the pilafs of the Middle East and the fried rice of many Asian and South-East Asian countries. It is used in soups, salads, sweets, casseroles and curries. Rice has the ability to absorb other flavours, becoming what we want it to be. It is the most versatile of all grains and has been given the title of King of Kernels.

VARIETIES OF RICE

There are about 60,000 varieties of rice cultivated around the world, but the most significant factor from the cook's standpoint is the shape and length of the grain and its starch content.

ARBORIO RICE: Has a large, plump, rounded kernel. It is grown in the Po Valley in Northern Italy. It has a high starch content, which gives the distinctive creamy texture to Italian risottos. It is also good for inclusion in soups and makes a creamy rice pudding.

BASMATI RICE: Has a long, narrow kernel and is prized for its fragrance and nutty flavour. Originating in the foothills of the Himalayas, it is the preferred rice for Indian cooking. Its flavour and firm yet tender texture when cooked has made it popular with all cuisines.

LONG-GRAIN RICE: Many varieties are produced under this title. They all have a long, thin kernel and remain well separated, dry and fluffy when cooked. Its flavour is somewhat bland but its features make it the best choice for rice salads and for pilafs, as it absorbs other flavours well.

SHORT- AND MEDIUM-GRAIN RICE: These varieties have a short, round kernel, some shorter than others. When cooked they are moist, slightly sticky and tend to cling. These are the rices to eat with chopsticks. They have a higher starch content than long-grained rice varieties, which makes them suitable for thickening soups; to use in stuffings for chicken, stuffed tomatoes and capsicums (peppers) and vine leaf rolls; for moulded rice and sushi, rice cakes and patties; and, of course, a good rice custard or creamed rice.

BROWN RICE: Most of the above varieties may be purchased in the brown form. Brown rice has the tough outer hull removed only, leaving the bran layer which

covers the grain intact. Because of the presence of this bran, brown rice is more nutritious than white and it takes longer to cook.

GLUTINOUS RICE: A short-grained rice which when boiled becomes sweet and sticky, with an appealing flavour. It is used as an ingredient in Asian sweets and snacks but is not used for savoury dishes or as an accompanying table rice. Polished and unpolished black rice varieties are available.

COOKING RICE

How much?

1 cup of raw rice gives 3 cups of cooked rice. This quantity will serve 3–4 people.

Some cook rice by guesswork, which can make it difficult to gain a good result. Based on how many serves you need to produce, calculate the amount of raw rice needed to be cooked, (eg, for 6 serves of cooked rice, 1–1$^1/_2$ cups of raw rice will need to be cooked) and use one of the following methods.

BOILING METHODS

RAPID BOIL METHOD: Rice is cooked in a large quantity of boiling, salted water for 12–15 minutes (30–35 minutes for brown rice) until soft but still firm at the core. It is then drained through a strainer. Use about 2 litres (3 pints) of water to 1 cup raw rice. This method ensures a separated, fluffy, dry grain; however, the liquid discarded takes some nutrients with it.

ABSORPTION METHOD: Rice is cooked in a measured quantity of water, which will be absorbed by the rice. There is no loose water left to drain out, so no nutrients are lost. Bring 2 cups (250 ml, 8 fl oz) water and a little salt to the boil and slowly stir in 1 cup rice. Cover tightly with a lid and turn down the heat to as low as possible. Simmer for 20 minutes without disturbing. Turn off heat or remove from hot plate and stand, without removing the lid, for 5–8 minutes; the rice will plump up in the stored heat. Fluff up with a fork and serve immediately. Brown rice will need 45 minutes cooking and 10 minutes standing time.

PILAF METHOD: Heat 2 tablespoons olive oil, ghee or butter in a heavy-based saucepan over moderate heat. Add 1 cup of rice and stir to coat all grains. Continue to stir over the heat for about 2–3 minutes until the rice has a rosy tinge. Add 1½ cups (375 ml, 12 fl oz) boiling water and a little salt. Reduce heat to low and cover with a tight lid. Simmer 15 minutes for white rice and 40 minutes for brown. Turn off heat and stand, covered, for 5–8 minutes. Fluff up with a fork and serve.

MICROWAVE METHOD: It will take the same amount of time to cook rice in the microwave as it will on the top of the stove. For small amounts it is convenient to use the microwave, for large amounts it is best to use a saucepan. Adding hot water to the rice will reduce time by about 5 minutes. Place 1 cup of rice and 2 cups (500 ml, 16 fl oz) hot water in a large microwave-safe container. Cook on 100% power for 10–12 minutes. Stand, covered, for 5 minutes before removing cover.

REHEATING RICE

1 Place the cooked rice in a colander over simmering water and heat through.
2 Place the cooked cold rice in a microwave-safe dish, sprinkle with a little water and cover. Heat for 4–6 minutes on high power, depending on the amount of rice and the wattage of the microwave oven.

PREPARING RICE FOR FRIED RICE

For a good result when making fried rice, the cooked rice must be free of moisture.

1 Cook the rice in advance, preferably the day before, for it takes time to remove the moisture.
2 Boil the rice by the rapid boil method, rinse well with cold water and leave to drain very well.
3 Spread the rice onto a shallow tray and place uncovered in the refrigerator for at least 2 hours; the cold air has a drying effect. Rake over the rice after 1 hour to bring the underside to the top.
4 For quick convenience keep prepared rice for frying in sealed bags in the freezer. It may be used in the frozen state.

FLAVOURING RICE

It is easy to flavour the rice while cooking it to make tasty accompaniments.

Quantities:
1 cup (200 g, 7 oz) long- or medium-grain rice
1 cup (250 ml, 8 fl oz) liquid

Method used:
Absorption method: Place all ingredients in a saucepan and bring to the boil, stirring occasionally. Turn down heat to a simmer, cover with a lid and simmer for 20 minutes. Stand, covered, for 5–8 minutes before removing lid to serve.

Apple rice:
1 cup rice, 1 cup (250 ml, 8 fl oz) apple juice, 1 cup (250 ml, 8 fl oz) stock or water, 1 tart apple (finely diced), salt to taste. Serve with pork.

Lemon rice:
1 cup rice, 1$\frac{1}{3}$ cups (440 ml, 14 fl oz) water, 4 tablespoons lemon juice, 1 teaspoon grated lemon rind, 1 cup (250 ml, 8 fl oz) stock or water, 2 tablespoons sultanas, salt to taste. Serve with fish.

Orange rice:
1 cup rice, 1 cup (250 ml, 8 fl oz) orange juice, 2 teaspoons grated orange rind, 1 cup (250 ml, 8 fl oz) stock or water, 2 tablespoons sultanas, salt to taste. Serve with chicken.

Onion rice:
1 cup rice, $\frac{1}{2}$ packet dried onion soup mix, 2 cups (500 ml, 16 fl oz) water. No salt needed. Serve with steaks.

Tomatoes yemistes

INGREDIENTS

12 medium-sized ripe
  tomatoes, washed
2 teaspoons sugar
salt and pepper
extra $1/2$ teaspoon sugar
$1/2$ cup (125 ml, 4 fl oz) olive oil
1 large onion, finely chopped
45 g (1 $1/2$ oz) pine nuts
$1 1/4$ cups (280 g, 9 oz) short-
  grain rice
75 g (2 $1/2$ oz) currants
$1 1/2$ cups (375 ml, 12 fl oz) hot
  water
2 tablespoons chopped flat-
  leaf parsley
2 tablespoons chopped mint
makes 12

1 Slice the top of each tomato almost through. Flip
   back the lid and scoop out the pulp with a teaspoon.
   Sprinkle each cavity with a pinch of sugar, place in
   a baking dish and set aside. Into a saucepan, place
   tomato pulp with salt, pepper and $1/2$ teaspoon sugar.
   Simmer until pulp is soft. Press through a sieve,
   discard seeds. Set purée aside.

2 In a saucepan, heat 4 tablespoons oil and fry the onion
   until soft. Add pine nuts and stir 2 minutes. Add rice,
   stir a little to coat grains. Add currants, hot water,
   parsley, mint and $1/2$ cup (125 ml, 4 fl oz) tomato purée.
   Bring to the boil, turn down heat, cover and simmer
   gently 10–12 minutes, until all liquid is absorbed.

3 Preheat oven to 180°C (350° F, gas mark 4). Spoon rice
   mixture into tomatoes, allowing a little room for rice
   to swell. Replace lid. Pour remaining tomato purée
   over the tomatoes and add about $1/2$ cup (125 ml,
   4 fl oz) water to the dish.

4 Spoon remaining oil over the tomatoes and place,
   uncovered, into oven for 40–60 minutes or until rice
   is tender. Check liquid – if drying out, add a little extra
   water. Serve tomatoes with their sauce.

PREPARATION TIME
25 minutes

COOKING TIME
1 hour

NUTRITIONAL VALUE PER SERVE   FAT **7.1** G   CARBOHYDRATE **5.5** G   PROTEIN **1.4** G

Crispy rolls

INGREDIENTS

1 cup (220 g, 7$^1/_2$ oz) short-grain brown
    rice, cooked
125 g (4 oz) cooked chicken,
    finely chopped
4 spring onions (green onions),
    chopped
1 carrot, grated
30 g (1 oz) bean sprouts
30 g (1 oz) button mushrooms,
    chopped
4 canned water chestnuts, drained
    and chopped
1 tablespoon oyster sauce
1 tablespoon soy sauce
2 teaspoons white wine
1 teaspoon sugar
$^1/_4$ teaspoon sesame oil
24 spring roll or wonton wrappers,
    each 12.5 cm (5in) square
vegetable oil for deep-frying
makes about 24

1 In a bowl, place rice, chicken, spring onions
(green onions), carrot, bean sprouts,
mushrooms, chestnuts, oyster and soy sauce,
wine, sugar and sesame oil and mix well to
combine. Take a spring roll wrapper, place on
work surface with a corner tip to the front.
Place a tablespoon of filling in the centre of
each wrapper, fold one corner over filling,
then tuck in the sides and roll up, sealing with
water.

2 Heat vegetable oil in a deep frying pan to
180°C (350°F, gas mark 4) or until a cube of
bread browns in 50 seconds. Cook a few rolls
at a time for 3–4 minutes or until golden.
Remove rolls with a slotted spoon, drain on
absorbent paper and serve immediately.

PREPARATION TIME
20 minutes

COOKING TIME
20 minutes

NUTRITIONAL VALUE PER SERVE	FAT 28.1 G	CARBOHYDRATE 11.2 G	PROTEIN 5.3 G

Gingered Thai rice salad

INGREDIENTS

2 cups (400 g, 13 oz) long-grain rice
1.5 litres (2½ pints) water
5 spring onions (green onions),
    finely sliced on the diagonal
3 medium carrots, coarsely grated
4 baby bok choy (pak choi), chopped
2 kaffir lime leaves, finely sliced
2 handfuls coriander (cilantro),
    coarsely chopped
250 g (8 oz) roasted peanuts,
    chopped
1 tablespoon black sesame seeds
2 tablespoons chopped Thai basil
dressing
2 tablespoons vegetable or peanut oil
3 tablespoons lime juice
3 tablespoons Thai fish sauce
2 tablespoons palm sugar
2 tablespoons sweet chilli sauce
    (jalapeño jelly)
1 tablespoon finely chopped ginger
1 pinch chilli powder or cayenne
    pepper
salt and pepper to taste
serves 12

1 Cook rice in boiling salted water for 10–12 minutes or until tender. Drain and rinse thoroughly in cold water, then drain again. In a bowl, whisk together dressing ingredients and set aside.

2 In a separate bowl, combine spring onions (green onions), carrots, bok choy (pak choi), lime leaves, coriander (cilantro), peanuts and sesame seeds.

3 Add the cooked rice and mix well. Toss thoroughly with the dressing, add Thai basil and serve.

PREPARATION TIME
15 minutes

COOKING TIME
15 minutes

NUTRITIONAL VALUE PER SERVE	FAT 7.5 G	CARBOHYDRATE 21 G	PROTEIN 5.2 G

Fish stuffed with Arabic rice

INGREDIENTS

1.2–1.5 kg (2¹/₂–3 lb) whole fish, such
  as snapper, bream, sea bass or red
  mullet, cleaned and scaled
Arabic rice stuffing
2 teaspoons vegetable oil
1 onion, chopped
¹/₂ cup (100 g, 3¹/₂ oz) brown rice,
  cooked
2 tablespoons pine nuts
2 tablespoons currants
2 tablespoons chopped fresh parsley
¹/₂ teaspoon ground allspice
2 tablespoons lemon juice
freshly ground black pepper
serves 4

PREPARATION TIME
10 minutes

COOKING TIME
25 minutes

1 To make stuffing, heat oil in a frying pan over a medium heat. Add onion and fry
   for 4 minutes or until onion is golden. In a bowl, combine onion, rice, pine nuts,
   currants, parsley, allspice, lemon juice and pepper. Set aside.

2 Wash fish and dry with absorbent paper. Make cavity of fish larger by cutting along
   the backbone almost to the tail. Fill cavity with stuffing and secure opening with a
   bamboo skewer.

3 Preheat oven to 180°C (350°F, gas mark 4). Place fish in the centre of a sheet of oiled
   aluminium foil. Lift edges to enclose fish and seal with a double fold. Place on a
   baking rack in a baking dish, adding hot water to the dish. Bake in oven for
   25 minutes or until flesh flakes when tested.

NUTRITIONAL VALUE PER SERVE	FAT **3.1** G	CARBOHYDRATE **5.6** G	PROTEIN **17.7** G

Lobster Provençale

INGREDIENTS

1¼ cups (250 g, 8 oz) long-grain rice
4 tablespoons butter
1 teaspoon freshly crushed garlic
2 spring onions (green onions),
  chopped
310 g (10 oz) canned tomatoes,
  chopped
salt and cracked black peppercorns
pinch of saffron
1 large cooked lobster or 4 cooked
  lobster tails
4 tablespoons brandy
½ bunch fresh chives, chopped, for
  garnish
1 lemon

serves 4

1 Boil the rice 12–13 minutes or until tender, drain and keep hot. In a shallow frying pan, melt butter over a moderate heat. Add garlic, spring onions (green onions), tomatoes, salt, pepper and saffron. Cook about 2 minutes until onions are translucent.

2 Remove meat from lobster and cut into large pieces. Add lobster meat to pan and flame with the brandy. Cook gently until lobster is heated through.

3 On serving plate, place rice and sprinkle with chives. Arrange the lobster on the rice and spoon over the sauce from the pan. Serve with lemon wedges.

PREPARATION TIME
15 minutes

COOKING TIME
15 minutes

NUTRITIONAL VALUE PER SERVE   FAT **4.2** G   CARBOHYDRATE **20** G   PROTEIN **10.3** G

Seafood paella

INGREDIENTS

1 tablespoon olive oil
2 onions, chopped
2 cloves garlic, crushed
375 g (12 oz) long-grain white rice
1 litre (1²/₃ pints) chicken stock
pinch saffron threads
250 g (8 oz) calamari (squid) rings
185 g (6 oz) smoked ham, sliced
250 g (8 oz) chorizo sausage, sliced
440 g (14 oz) can peeled tomatoes,
   undrained and mashed
315 g (10 oz) white fish fillets, cubed
250 g (8 oz) green medium-sized prawns
   (shrimps), shelled and deveined
500 g (1 lb) mussels, scrubbed and
   beards removed
125 g (4 oz) peas
serves 6

1 In a paella pan or large deep-frying pan, heat oil over a medium heat. Add onions and garlic and cook, stirring, for 3 minutes, until onions are soft. Add rice and cook, stirring, for 4–5 minutes until rice is translucent.

2 Stir stock, saffron, calamari (squid), ham, sausage and tomatoes into pan and bring to the boil. Reduce heat and simmer, stirring occasionally, for 25 minutes or until rice is tender and liquid is absorbed.

3 Place fish, prawns (shrimps), mussels and peas on top of rice mixture, add a little extra hot stock or water if needed. Reduce heat to low, cover and cook for 10 minutes or until seafood and peas are cooked. Discard any mussels that do not open after 5 minutes. Serve immediately.

PREPARATION TIME
15 minutes

COOKING TIME
45 minutes

| NUTRITIONAL VALUE PER SERVE | FAT 3.1 G | CARBOHYDRATE 9.4 G | PROTEIN 8.3 G |

Nasi goreng

INGREDIENTS

250 g (8 oz) long-grain rice
1 litre (1²/₃ pints) boiling water
1 teaspoon ground turmeric
3 tablespoons vegetable oil
1 bunch spring onions (green onions),
   thinly sliced
2.5 cm fresh root ginger, finely
   chopped
1–2 red chillies, deseeded and thinly
   sliced
225 g (7¹/₂ oz) pork fillet, thinly sliced
2 cloves garlic, crushed
3 tablespoons soy sauce, or to taste
200 g (7 oz) cooked peeled prawns
   (shrimps), defrosted if frozen and
   thoroughly dried
juice of ¹/₂ lemon
coriander (cilantro) for garnish
serves 4

1 Cook the rice in boiling salted water, with turmeric added, for 12–15 minutes. Drain, then spread on to a large flat baking tray. Leave to cool for 1 hour or until completely cold, fluffing up occasionally with a fork.

2 Heat 2 tablespoons of the oil in a wok or heavy-based frying pan. Add half the spring onions (green onions), the ginger and chillies and stir-fry over a low heat for 2–3 minutes until softened. Add the remaining oil and increase the heat to high. Add the pork and garlic and stir-fry for 3 minutes.

3 Add the rice in 3 batches, stirring after each addition to mix well with the other ingredients. Add the soy sauce and prawns (shrimps) and stir-fry for 2–3 minutes until hot. Transfer to a bowl and mix in the lemon juice. Sprinkle with the remaining spring onions (green onions) and garnish with coriander (cilantro).

PREPARATION TIME
10 minutes

COOKING TIME
15–20 minutes

NUTRITIONAL VALUE PER SERVE	FAT **6.5** G	CARBOHYDRATE **20** G	PROTEIN **11.7** G

Malay beef risotto

INGREDIENTS

2 tablespoons sesame or peanut oil
6 spring onions (green onions), finely
   chopped
4 cloves garlic, crushed
1 teaspoon cumin
$^1/_2$–1 teaspoon red chilli, finely
   chopped
500 g (1 lb) lean beef, cubed
1 litre ($1^2/_3$ pints) hot beef or vegetable
   stock
400 g (13 oz) long-grain rice
100 ml ($3^1/_2$ fl oz) rice wine
6 tablespoons chunky peanut butter
2 tablespoons soy sauce
$^1/_2$ Chinese cabbage, finely shredded
1 tablespoon lime juice
90 g (3 oz) roasted peanuts, chopped
serves 4–6

PREPARATION TIME
15 minutes

COOKING TIME
**40 minutes, plus
5 minutes standing**

1 Heat the sesame or peanut oil in a large heavy-based saucepan. Add
   the spring onions (green onions), garlic, cumin and chilli. Sauté for
   2 minutes, add the beef cubes and sauté for about 5 minutes until
   browned. Add 1 cup of stock, turn down heat and simmer for 15 minutes.

2 Add the rice, the rice wine, peanut butter, soy sauce and the remaining
   stock. Bring to the boil, add the shredded cabbage, reduce heat, cover
   and simmer for 15 minutes. Turn off heat and stand, covered, for
   5 minutes before serving.

3 Pile the risotto into individual bowls, sprinkle with lime juice and
   chopped roasted peanuts.

NUTRITIONAL VALUE PER SERVE	FAT 7.5 G	CARBOHYDRATE 13 G	PROTEIN 7.9 G

Rice with chicken livers, pine nuts and currants

INGREDIENTS

500 g (1 lb) chicken livers
75 g (2¹/₂ oz) butter
12 spring onions (green onions),
  chopped
1¹/₂ cups (330 g, 11 oz)
  short-grain rice
750 ml (1¹/₄ pints) chicken stock
2 handfuls parsley, chopped
100 g (3¹/₂ oz) pine nuts
100 g (3¹/₂ oz) currants
serves 8

PREPARATION TIME
10 minutes

COOKING TIME
35 minutes, plus
10 minutes standing

1 Wash chicken livers, and remove any sinew. Chop livers in half.

2 Heat butter in a large saucepan and sauté the spring onions (green onions) for 5 minutes until tender. Add the chicken livers and sauté for a few minutes until they change colour.

3 Add the rice and chicken stock to the saucepan and bring to the boil. Simmer with the lid on, stirring occasionally, for approximately 25 minutes. Add the parsley, pine nuts and currants, stir through the rice, and cook a further 3 minutes. Turn off heat and stand covered for 10 minutes.

NUTRITIONAL VALUE PER SERVE	FAT 7.6 G	CARBOHYDRATE 16.2 G	PROTEIN 6.7 G

Risotto of tomato and basil

INGREDIENTS

1 tablespoon butter
1 tablespoon olive oil
2 cloves garlic, minced
1 onion, finely chopped
400 g (13 oz) arborio rice
$^1/_2$ cup (125 ml, 4 fl oz) dry white wine
1 litre (1 $^2/_3$ pints) vegetable or chicken
   stock, simmering
4 roma tomatoes, halved lengthwise
8 sun-dried tomatoes, chopped
20 fresh basil leaves, cut into strips
30 g (1 oz) parmesan cheese, grated
2 tablespoons mascarpone cheese
salt and freshly ground black pepper
extra basil leaves for garnish
serves 4–6

PREPARATION TIME
5 minutes

COOKING TIME
30 minutes

1 Heat the butter and oil in a large saucepan. Add the garlic and onion and sauté until the onion is transparent. Add the rice and stir to coat. Add the wine and stir until absorbed.

2 Add half the stock a ladle at a time, stirring each addition until absorbed before adding the next ladle of stock.

3 Add the roma tomatoes, sun-dried tomatoes and basil, and stir well. Continue to add stock until the rice is still firm to bite and all the liquid has been absorbed.

4 Remove the saucepan from the heat and stir through the parmesan, mascarpone, salt and pepper. Garnish with extra basil leaves and serve immediately.

NUTRITIONAL VALUE PER SERVE	FAT 3.2 G	CARBOHYDRATE 15 G	PROTEIN 2.6 G

Cheesy baked rice

INGREDIENTS

2 tablespoons butter or margarine
2 leeks, sliced
3 rashers bacon, chopped
$^1/_2$ red capsicum (pepper), finely
  chopped
60 g (2 oz) long-grain rice, cooked
1 $^1/_2$ cups (375 ml, 12 fl oz) milk
2 eggs, lightly beaten
$^1/_2$ teaspoon dry mustard
1 teaspoon worcestershire sauce
1 tablespoon mayonnaise
125 g (4 oz) mild cheddar, grated
2 tablespoons chopped fresh parsley
freshly ground black pepper
1 teaspoon paprika
serves 4

1 Preheat oven to 180°C (350°F, gas mark 4). Melt butter or margarine in a frying pan over a medium heat. Add leeks, bacon and capsicum (pepper) and cook, stirring, for 4–5 minutes or until leeks are soft and bacon is brown. Mix with the rice and spoon mixture into a lightly greased ovenproof dish, set aside.

2 Heat milk to hot but not boiling. In a bowl, whisk together the eggs, mustard, worcestershire sauce, mayonnaise, cheddar, parsley and black pepper.

3 Gradually whisk a few spoonfuls of hot milk into the egg mixture to temper the egg. Slowly pour in the remaining milk, while stirring.

4 Carefully pour the combined milk egg mixture into the ovenproof dish containing the rice and leeks.

5 Place dish in a baking dish with enough hot water to come halfway up the sides. Bake in oven for 28–30 minutes or until custard is firm.

PREPARATION TIME
10 minutes

COOKING TIME
40 minutes

NUTRITIONAL VALUE PER SERVE   FAT **11.1** G   CARBOHYDRATE **7.7** G   PROTEIN **8.9** G

Mushroom and black olive risotto

INGREDIENTS

15 g (¹/₂ oz) dried porcini mushrooms

200 ml (7 fl oz) boiling water

3 tablespoons olive oil

1 onion, chopped

250 g (8 oz) large field (open)
   mushrooms, chopped

250 g (8 oz) arborio rice

2 tablespoons pitted black olives,
   roughly chopped

450 ml (14 fl oz) vegetable stock

salt and black pepper

2 tablespoons black olive paste

60 g (2 oz) parmesan cheese
   cut from a block

serves 4

PREPARATION TIME
10 minutes, plus
20 minutes soaking

COOKING TIME
30 minutes, plus
5 minutes
standing

1 Cover the porcini with boiling water and leave to soak for 20 minutes. Drain, reserving the water, and set aside. Heat the oil in a large heavy-based saucepan. Add the onion and field mushrooms and fry for 4–5 minutes. Add the rice and stir to coat with the oil. Fry for 1–2 minutes.

2 Add the porcini and the reserved liquid to the rice with the olives and half the vegetable stock. Cover and simmer for 10 minutes or until the liquid has been absorbed, stirring occasionally.

3 Stir in 100 ml (3¹/₂ fl oz) of the remaining stock and cook for 5 minutes, covered, until absorbed. Add the remaining stock, salt, pepper and olive paste and cook for 5 minutes uncovered, stirring constantly. Remove from the heat and stand, covered, for 5 minutes. Transfer to a serving dish. Shave over the parmesan, using a vegetable peeler, and serve.

NUTRITIONAL VALUE PER SERVE	FAT 6.4 G	CARBOHYDRATE 17 G	PROTEIN 4.5 G

Risotto with baby spinach and gorgonzola

INGREDIENTS

1 litre (1 2/3 pints) chicken stock
2 tablespoons olive oil
2 cloves garlic, crushed
1 onion, finely chopped
2 cups (440 g, 14 oz) arborio rice
125 ml (4 fl oz) white wine
225 g (7 1/2 oz) baby spinach
225 g (7 1/2 oz) gorgonzola cheese, in
  small pieces
salt and freshly ground pepper
serves 6

PREPARATION TIME
10 minutes

COOKING TIME
25 minutes

1 In a saucepan, place stock and bring to the boil. Leave simmering. Heat oil
   in a large saucepan. Add garlic and onion, and cook for 5 minutes until soft.
   Add rice and stir until well coated. Pour in wine and cook until the liquid
   has been absorbed.

2 Add the stock to the saucepan, a ladle at a time, stirring continuously
   until liquid has been absorbed before adding the next ladle of stock. Keep
   adding stock this way, and stirring, until all the stock is used and the rice is
   cooked, but still a little firm to bite.

3 Add the spinach, gorgonzola, salt and pepper. Stir and cook until spinach is
   just wilted and cheese has melted. Serve immediately.

NUTRITIONAL VALUE PER SERVE	FAT 4.5 G	CARBOHYDRATE 16 G	PROTEIN 4.2 G

Indonesian rice

INGREDIENTS

1 ½ cups (300 g, 10 oz) basmati rice
2 tablespoons vegetable oil
2 onions, sliced
2 cloves garlic, crushed
2 teaspoons ground cumin
1 teaspoon ground coriander (cilantro)
2 teaspoons ground cardamom
2 fresh red chillies, chopped
2 ½ cups (625 ml, 1 pint) chicken stock
2 tablespoons honey
1 tablespoon soy sauce
2 spring onions (green onions),
   chopped
serves 4

PREPARATION TIME
8 minutes

COOKING TIME
25 minutes, plus
10 minutes standing

1 Place rice in a bowl, pour over enough hot water to cover and set aside to stand
   for 3 minutes. Drain.

2 Heat oil in a large frying pan. Add onions and garlic and stir-fry for 4–5 minutes
   or until onion is soft. Add cumin, coriander, cardamom, chillies and rice and
   stir-fry for 1 minute. In a bowl, combine stock, honey and soy sauce. Stir into
   rice mixture and bring to the boil. Reduce heat and boil gently for 10 minutes.

3 Turn heat to very low, cover and cook for 5 minutes longer. Remove from heat,
   stand, covered, 5–10 minutes to absorb remaining liquid. Stir in spring onions
   (green onions) and serve immediately.

NUTRITIONAL VALUE PER SERVE	FAT 3.2 G	CARBOHYDRATE 23.9 G	PROTEIN 2.5 G

Chilli fried rice

INGREDIENTS

2 teaspoons vegetable oil

2 fresh red chillies, chopped

1 tablespoon Thai red curry paste

2 onions, sliced

1½ cups (330 g, 11 oz) short-grain rice,
  cooked and cooled

125 g (4 oz) snake (yard-long) or
  green beans, chopped into 1.5 cm
  (½ in) pieces

125 g (4 oz) baby bok choy (pak choi),
  blanched

3 tablespoons lime juice

2 teaspoons Thai fish sauce

serves 4

1 Heat oil in a wok or frying pan over a high heat.
   Add chillies and curry paste and stir-fry for
   1 minute or until fragrant. Add onions and
   stir-fry for 3 minutes or until soft.

2 Add rice, beans and bok choy (pak choi) to pan
   and stir-fry for 4 minutes or until rice is heated
   through. Stir in lime juice and fish sauce.

PREPARATION TIME
**20 minutes including
cooked rice**

COOKING TIME
8 minutes

NUTRITIONAL VALUE PER SERVE	FAT **2.5** G	CARBOHYDRATE **11.7** G	PROTEIN **1.9** G

Fragrant pilaf

INGREDIENTS

large pinch of saffron strands
1 tablespoon boiling water
2 tablespoons butter
1 golden shallot, finely chopped
3 cardamom pods
1 cinnamon stick
1¼ cups (250 g, 8 oz) basmati rice,
   rinsed and drained
400 ml (13 fl oz) hot water
pinch salt
serves 4

1 Soak the saffron strands in 1 tablespoon water and set aside. Melt the butter in a large, heavy-based saucepan. Fry the shallot gently for 2 minutes or until softened. Add the cardamom pods, cinnamon and rice and mix well.

2 Add the hot water, salt and strain in the saffron liquid. Bring to the boil, then reduce the heat and cover the pan tightly. Simmer for 15 minutes or until the liquid has been absorbed and the rice is tender. Remove the cardamom pods and cinnamon stick before serving. Serve to accompany grilled fish or chicken.

PREPARATION TIME
5 minutes

COOKING TIME
20 minutes

NUTRITIONAL VALUE PER SERVE	FAT 0.1 G	CARBOHYDRATE 26 G	PROTEIN 0.1 G

Fried brown rice

INGREDIENTS

1¹/₂ cups (330 g, 11 oz) brown rice
2 tablespoons peanut oil
2 eggs, lightly beaten
2 celery stalks, chopped
1 red capsicum (pepper), chopped
2 cloves garlic, crushed
90 g (3 oz) frozen peas, cooked and
   drained
4 spring onions (green onions),
   chopped
1 tablespoon soy sauce
serves 4–6

PREPARATION TIME
10 minutes

COOKING TIME
**40 minutes, plus
3 hours refrigeration**

1 Cook rice in boiling water for about 30 minutes until tender. Drain well, spread
   out on a tray and refrigerate, uncovered, for 2 hours to dry out. Toss and
   re-spread after 1 hour.

2 Heat 2 teaspoons oil in a wok or small frying pan, swirl to coat the base. Pour
   eggs into pan and cook over a low heat, tilting the wok or pan to spread the egg.
   Cook until eggs are set. Tip out the omelette and slice thinly.

3 Heat remaining oil in the wok or large frying pan, add celery, capsicum (pepper)
   and garlic and stir-fry for 3–4 minutes. Add the rice and peas and stir-fry 2
   minutes to heat well. Add the egg strips, spring onions (green onions) and soy
   sauce and toss to distribute. Serve immediately.

NUTRITIONAL VALUE PER SERVE	FAT 7 G	CARBOHYDRATE 31 G	PROTEIN 5.8 G

Fig and rhubarb risotto

INGREDIENTS

400 ml (13 fl oz) orange juice
600 ml (1 pint) water
150 g (5 oz) sugar
8 ribs (sticks) rhubarb, red part only
2 tablespoons butter
10 dried figs, halved
400 g (13 oz) arborio rice
1 tablespoon mascarpone cheese
4–6 fresh figs
1 tablespoon brown sugar
serves 6–8

PREPARATION TIME
15 minutes

COOKING TIME
30 minutes

1 In a large pan, heat the orange juice, water and sugar, and simmer for
   10 minutes. Wash and slice the rhubarb into 2 cm (³/₄ in)pieces. In a separate
   pan, heat the butter. Add the rhubarb and figs and sauté for 3 minutes.

2 Add the rice and stir to coat. Begin adding the syrup and juice mixture, 1 cup
   (250 ml, 8 fl oz) at a time, stirring well until liquid is absorbed. Continue to
   add the syrup in the same manner until all the liquid has been absorbed and
   the rice is tender. Add the mascarpone cheese and stir well.

3 Cut the fresh figs in half and sprinkle a little brown sugar on each cut
   surface. Grill the fruit, sugar side up, about 2 minutes until caramelised.
   Serve atop the risotto in individual bowls.

NUTRITIONAL VALUE PER SERVE	FAT **2.9** G	CARBOHYDRATE **39** G	PROTEIN **2.5** G

Caramelised rice pudding with apricots

INGREDIENTS

75 g (2¹/₂ oz) short-grain rice
200 g (7 oz) caster sugar
2 vanilla beans (pods), 1 split in half
   lengthways
2 tablespoons unsalted butter
600 ml (1 pint) full-fat milk
145 ml (5 fl oz) double cream
2 strips lemon rind (zest)
250 g (8 oz) dried apricots
2 tablespoons lemon juice
1–2 tablespoons cointreau
serves 4

PREPARATION TIME
10 minutes, plus
1 hour cooling

COOKING TIME
60 minutes

1 Into a saucepan, put the rice and cover with water. Boil for 5 minutes and drain.
   Return the rice to the saucepan with 45 g (1¹/₂ oz) sugar, 1 of the vanilla beans (pods),
   butter and milk. Simmer for 45–60 minutes, stirring often, until thickened. Transfer
   to a bowl and cool for 20 minutes or until cold. Remove the vanilla bean (pod) and
   scrape the seeds into the rice. Discard the bean (pod). Whisk the cream until it forms
   soft peaks, then fold into the rice.

2 Meanwhile, put 100 g (3¹/₂ oz) of the sugar into a saucepan with the lemon,
   remaining vanilla bean (pod) and 200 ml (7 fl oz) of water. Heat, stirring, until
   the sugar dissolves. Add the apricots and cook for 10–15 minutes until syrup has
   thickened. Stir in the lemon juice and liqueur, stand to cool for 5 minutes.

3 Divide the apricots and their syrup between 4 ramekins. Top with the rice pudding
   and refrigerate for 1 hour. Preheat the grill to high. Sprinkle the puddings with the
   rest of the sugar. Grill for 1–2 minutes, until the sugar caramelises. Remove and
   stand 5 minutes to cool before serving.

NUTRITIONAL VALUE PER SERVE	FAT 8.7 G	CARBOHYDRATE 30 G	PROTEIN 2.8 G

Glossary

Al dente: Italian term to describe pasta and rice that are cooked until tender but still firm to the bite.

Bake blind: to bake pastry cases without their fillings. Line the raw pastry case with greaseproof paper and fill with raw rice or dried beans to prevent collapsed sides and puffed base. Remove paper and fill 5 minutes before completion of cooking time.

Baste: to spoon hot cooking liquid over food at intervals during cooking to moisten and flavour it.

Beat: to make a mixture smooth with rapid and regular motions using a spatula, wire whisk or electric mixer; to make a mixture light and smooth by enclosing air.

Beurre manié: equal quantities of butter and flour mixed together to a smooth paste and stirred bit by bit into a soup, stew or sauce while on the heat to thicken. Stop adding when desired thickness results.

Bind: to add egg or a thick sauce to hold ingredients together when cooked.

Blanch: to plunge some foods into boiling water for less than a minute and immediately plunge into iced water. This is to brighten the colour of some vegetables and to remove skin from tomatoes and nuts.

Blend: to mix 2 or more ingredients thoroughly together; do not confuse with blending in an electric blender.

Boil: to cook in a liquid brought to boiling point and kept there.

Boiling point: when bubbles rise continually and break over the entire surface of the liquid, reaching a temperature of 100°C (212°F). In some cases food is held at this high temperature for a few seconds then heat is turned to low for slower cooking. See *simmer*.

Bouquet garni: a bundle of several herbs tied together with string for easy removal, placed into pots of stock, soups and stews for flavour. A few sprigs of fresh thyme, parsley and bay leaf are used. Can be purchased in sachet form for convenience.

Caramelise: to heat sugar in a heavy-based pan until it liquefies and develops a caramel colour. Vegetables such as blanched carrots and sautéed onions may be sprinkled with sugar and caramelised.

Chill: to place in the refrigerator or stir over ice until cold.

Clarify: to make a liquid clear by removing sediments and impurities. To melt fat and remove any sediment.

Coat: to dust or roll food items in flour to cover the surface before the food is cooked. Also, to coat in flour, egg and breadcrumbs.

Cool: to stand at room temperature until some or all heat is removed, eg cool a little, cool completely.

Cream: to make creamy and fluffy by working the mixture with the back of a wooden spoon; usually refers to creaming butter and sugar or margarine. May also be done with an electric mixer.

Croutons: small cubes of bread, toasted or fried, used as an addition to salads or as a garnish to soups and stews.

Crudités: raw vegetable sticks served with a dipping sauce.

Crumb: to coat foods in flour, egg and breadcrumbs to form a protective coating for foods which are fried. Also adds flavour and texture and enhances appearance.

Cube: to cut into small pieces with six even sides, eg cubes of meat.

Cut in: to combine fat, such as butter or shortening, and flour using 2 knives scissor-fashion or a pastry blender, to make pastry.

Deglaze: to dissolve dried-out cooking juices left on the base and sides of a roasting dish or frying pan. Add a little water, wine or stock, scrape and stir over heat until dissolved. Resulting liquid is used to make a flavoursome gravy or added to a sauce or casserole.

Degrease: to skim fat from the surface of cooking liquids, eg stocks, soups, casseroles.

Dice: to cut into small cubes.

Dredge: to heavily coat with icing sugar, sugar, flour or cornflour.

Dressing: a mixture added to completed dishes to add moisture and flavour, eg salads, cooked vegetables.

Drizzle: to pour in a fine thread-like stream moving over a surface.

Egg wash: beaten egg with milk or water used to brush over pastry, bread dough or biscuits to give a sheen and golden brown colour.

Essence: a strong flavouring liquid, usually made by distillation. Only a few drops are needed to flavour.

Fillet: a piece of prime meat, fish or poultry which is boneless or has all bones removed.

Flake: to separate cooked fish into flakes, removing any bones and skin, using 2 forks.

Flame: to ignite warmed alcohol over food or to pour into a pan with food, ignite, then serve.

Flute: to make decorative indentations around the pastry rim before baking.

Fold in: combining of a light, whisked or creamed mixture with other ingredients. Add a portion of the other ingredients at a time and mix using a gentle circular motion, over and under the mixture so that air will not be lost. Use a metal spoon or spatula.

Glaze: to brush or coat food with a liquid that will give the finished product a glossy appearance, and on baked products, a golden brown colour.

Grease: to rub the surface of a metal or heatproof dish with oil or fat, to prevent the food from sticking.

Herbed butter: softened butter mixed with finely chopped fresh herbs and re-chilled. Used to serve on grilled meats and fish.

Hors d'oeuvre: small savoury foods served as an appetiser, popularly known today as 'finger food'.

Infuse: to steep foods in a liquid until the liquid absorbs their flavour.

Joint: to cut poultry and game into serving pieces by dividing at the joint.

Julienne: to cut some food, eg vegetables and processed meats, into fine strips the length of matchsticks. Used in salads or as a garnish to cooked dishes.

Knead: to work a yeast dough in a pressing, stretching and folding motion with the heel of the hand until smooth and elastic to develop the gluten strands. Non-yeast doughs should be lightly and quickly handled as gluten development is not desired.

Line: to cover the inside of a baking tin with paper for the easy removal of the cooked product from the baking tin.

Macerate: to stand fruit in a syrup, liqueur or spirit to give added flavour.

Marinade: a flavoured liquid, into which food is placed for some time to give it flavour and to tenderise. Marinades include an acid ingredient such as vinegar or wine, oil and seasonings.

Mask: to evenly cover cooked food portions with a sauce, mayonnaise or savoury jelly.

Pan-fry: to fry foods in a small amount of fat or oil, sufficient to coat the base of the pan.

Parboil: to boil until partially cooked. The food is then finished by some other method.

Pare: to peel the skin from vegetables and fruit. 'Peel' is the popular term but 'pare' is the name given to the knife used; paring knife.

Pit: to remove stones or seeds from olives, cherries, dates.

Pith: the white lining between the rind and flesh of oranges, grapefruit and lemons.

Pitted: the olives, cherries, dates etc. with the stone removed, eg purchase pitted dates.

Poach: to simmer gently in enough hot liquid to almost cover the food so its shape will be retained.

Pound: to flatten meats with a meat mallet; to reduce to a paste or small particles with a mortar and pestle.

Simmer: to cook in liquid just below boiling point at about 96°C (205°F) with small bubbles rising gently to the surface.

Skim: to remove fat or froth from the surface of simmering food.

Stock: the liquid produced when meat, poultry, fish or vegetables have been simmered in water to extract the flavour. Used as a base for soups, sauces, casseroles etc. Convenience stock products are available.

Sweat: to cook sliced onions or vegetables in a small amount of butter in a covered pan over low heat, to soften them and release flavour without colouring.

Conversions

Measurements differ from country to country, so it's important to understand what the differences are. This Measurements Guide gives you simple 'at-a-glance' information for using the recipes in this book, wherever you may be.

Cooking is not an exact science – minor variations in measurements won't make a difference to your cooking.

EQUIPMENT

There is a difference in the size of measuring cups used internationally, but the difference is minimal (only 2–3 teaspoons). We use the standard metric measurements in our recipes:

1 teaspoon.....5 ml   1 tablespoon.....20 ml
1/2 cup.....125 ml   1 cup.....250 ml
4 cups.....1 litre

Measuring cups come in sets of one cup (250 ml), 1/2 cup (125 ml), 1/3 cup (80 ml) and 1/4 cup (60 ml). Use these for measuring liquids and certain dry ingredients.

Measuring spoons come in a set of four and should be used for measuring dry and liquid ingredients.

When using cup or spoon measures, always make them level (unless the recipe indicates otherwise).

DRY VERSUS WET INGREDIENTS

While this system of measures is consistent for liquids, it's more difficult to quantify dry ingredients. For instance, one level cup equals: 200 g of brown sugar; 210 g of caster sugar; and 110 g of icing sugar.

When measuring dry ingredients such as flour, don't push the flour down or shake it into the cup. It is best just to spoon the flour in until it reaches the desired amount. When measuring liquids, use a clear vessel indicating metric levels.

Always use medium eggs (55–60 g) when eggs are required in a recipe.

OVEN

Your oven should always be at the right temperature before placing the food in it to be cooked. Note that if your oven doesn't have a fan you may need to cook food for a little longer.

MICROWAVE

It is difficult to give an exact cooking time for microwave cooking. It is best to watch what you are cooking closely to monitor its progress.

STANDING TIME

Many foods continue to cook when you take them out of the oven or microwave. If a recipe states that the food needs to 'stand' after cooking, be sure not to overcook the dish.

CAN SIZES

The can sizes available in your supermarket or grocery store may not be the same as specified in the recipe. Don't worry if there is a small variation in size – it's unlikely to make a difference to the end result.

dry		liquids	
metric (grams)	imperial (ounces)	metric (millilitres)	imperial (fluid ounces)
		30 ml	1 fl oz
30 g	1 oz	60 ml	2 fl oz
60 g	2 oz	90 ml	3 fl oz
90 g	3 oz	100 ml	3 1/2 fl oz
100 g	3 1/2 oz	125 ml	4 fl oz
125 g	4 oz	150 ml	5 fl oz
150 g	5 oz	190 ml	6 fl oz
185 g	6 oz	250 ml	8 fl oz
200 g	7 oz	300 ml	10 fl oz
250 g	8 oz	500 ml	16 fl oz
280 g	9 oz	600 ml	20 fl oz (1 pint)*
315 g	10 oz	1000 ml (1 litre)	32 fl oz
330 g	11 oz		
370 g	12 oz		
400 g	13 oz		
440 g	14 oz		
470 g	15 oz		
500 g	16 oz (1 lb)		
750 g	24 oz (1 1/2 lb)		
1000 g (1 kg)	32 oz (2 lb)		*Note: an American pint is 16 fl oz.

cooking temperatures	°C (celsius)	°F (fahrenheit)	gas mark
very slow	120	250	1/2
slow	150	300	2
moderately slow	160	315	2–3
moderate	180	350	4
moderately hot	190	375	5
	200	400	6
hot	220	425	7
very hot	230	450	8
	240	475	9
	250	500	10

Index

Essential COOKING SERIES

COMPREHENSIVE, STEP-BY-STEP COOKING

Essential COOKING SERIES
COMPREHENSIVE, STEP-BY-STEP COOKING
Baking

Essential COOKING SERIES
COMPREHENSIVE, STEP-BY-STEP COOKING
Chicken Meals

Essential COOKING SERIES
COMPREHENSIVE, STEP-BY-STEP COOKING
Salads & Greens

Essential COOKING SERIES
COMPREHENSIVE, STEP-BY-STEP COOKING
Soups & Hors D'Oeuvres

Essential COOKING SERIES
COMPREHENSIVE, STEP-BY-STEP COOKING
Meat Dishes

Essential COOKING SERIES
COMPREHENSIVE, STEP-BY-STEP COOKING
Finger Food

Essential COOKING SERIES
COMPREHENSIVE, STEP-BY-STEP COOKING
Pasta Dishes

Essential COOKING SERIES
COMPREHENSIVE, STEP-BY-STEP COOKING
Grilling & Barbecuing

Essential COOKING SERIES
COMPREHENSIVE, STEP-BY-STEP COOKING
Rice & Risotto

Essential COOKING SERIES
COMPREHENSIVE, STEP-BY-STEP COOKING
Vegetarian Dishes

Essential COOKING SERIES
COMPREHENSIVE, STEP-BY-STEP COOKING
Asian Dishes

Essential COOKING SERIES
COMPREHENSIVE, STEP-BY-STEP COOKING
Stir-Fry